ESTATE PUBLICATIONS

TTINGBOURNE · FAVERSI

SDOWN-ON-SEA · MINSTER · SHEERNES

G000277767

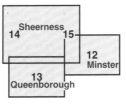

14 Sheerness **15**				
		12 Minster		
13 Queenborough				

Eastchurch **10**

11 Leysdown -on-Sea

16 Upchurch

Newington **17**

3 Kemsley

SITTINGBOURNE

4   **5**   **6**

Bapchild

Teynham **7**

Oare **7**

FAVERSHAM

8   **9**

Boughton **10** Street

Scale of street plans: 4 Inches to 1 Mile (unless otherwise stated)

═══ Motorway	Every effort has been made to verify the accuracy of information in this book but the publishers cannot accept responsibility for expense or loss caused by an error or omission. Information that will be of assistance to the user of the maps will be welcomed.	∿ Stream / River
═══ 'A' Road / Dual		∿ Canal
═══ 'B' Road / Dual		→ One-way Street
═══ Minor Road / Dual		🄿 Car Park
═══ Track		🄲 Public Convenience
▨▨▨ Pedestrianized	The representation on these maps of a road, track or path is no evidence of the existence of a right of way.	🄸 Tourist Information
▬■▬ Railway / Station		+ Place of Worship
- - - Footpath		● Post Office

eet plans prepared and published by ESTATE PUBLICATIONS, Bridewell House, TENTERDEN, KENT.
The Publishers acknowledge the co-operation of the local authorities
of towns represented in this atlas.

OS Ordnance Survey® This product includes mapping data licensed from Ordnance Survey®
with the permission of the Controller of Her Majesty's Stationery Office.

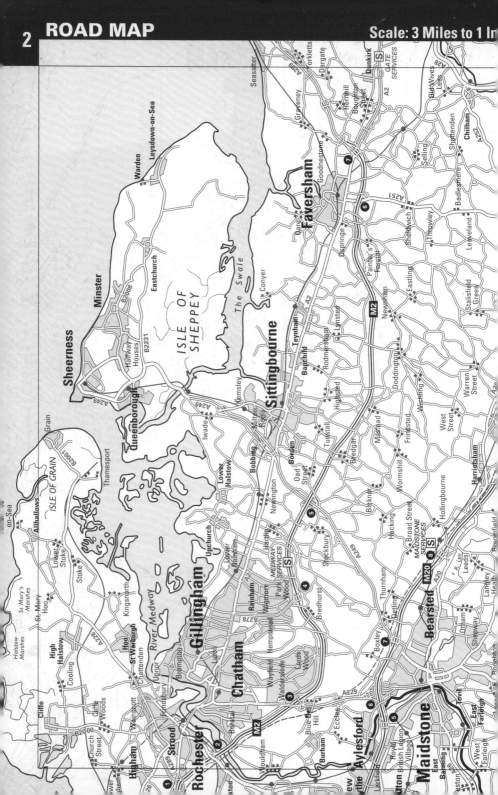

A B C D

1

2

3

4

5

6

JTHLANDS OSPITAL

ROOK LANE

COLD HARBOUR LANE

BOBBING HILL

WAY

Bobbing Court

bbing

Services

GALENA CL

HARBAR DR

SONO

TOURMALIN DR

B2006

STAPLEHURST RD

Milton Regis

SONORA WY

GALENA CL

STAPLEHURST RD

Hill Farm

KEYCOL HILL

A2

SHEPPEY

School

Sports Grnd

HILTON

NORWOOD WK

NORWOOD

WELLINGTON WK

CLIVE RD

GORDON DRIVE

WOOLLET

SIMPSON WK

GIBRALTAR

GAYHURST

DRIVE

Chalkwell

A249

CHESTNUT STREET

SCHOOL LANE

STREET

KEY STREET LONDON

Key Street

CHERRYFIELDS

GROVE PARK AV

BRIAR

The Grove Park

Cricket Ground

SANDFORD

CHATSWORTH

RUSHENDEN DR

LONSDALE DR

WILTON TER

NEWLANDS AV

WESTLANDS AV

KENILWORTH DR

WENTWORTH DR

WARWICK CRES

PRENTIS CL

SOMERSET CL

SYDNEY

PERTH

CANBERRA AV

ADELAIDE GDS

HOBART

BRISBANE AV

NAPIER

DUNEDIN

HAMILTON

OAKDEN

BORDEN

RUSSELL CL

AUCKLAND DRIVE

CRYALLS DRIVE

WALNUT TREE DR

LYDBROOK CL

HOMEWOOD

Sch

SILVERDALE RD

BERKELEY GRO

WINDSOR

INKHEAD QUAY

COURT

HEVER RD

KENT

HILL

Westlands School

CRYALLS LANE

WISES LANE

BRIAR ROAD

LA Sch

SCHOOL LANE

MUNSGORE

Limepits Cross

Sunnyhill

BORDEN LANE

RIDDLES LANE

Adult Education Centre

WESTERHAM RD

CHAPEL WELL

WESTERHAM

GRAYLING RD

COLLEGE RD

MINTERNE

WOODS

+

Borden

THE STREET

HOMESTEAD VW

MOUNTVIEW

BARN CL

MOUNT STREET

COLPINS LA

BANNISTER HILL

THE RISE

Harmans Corner

ROAD

Pond Farm

FARM

POND

DELIGHT HILL

HEARTS

HEARTS DELIGHT ROAD

STERLING

STERLIN

STERLING

HALES RD

A B C D

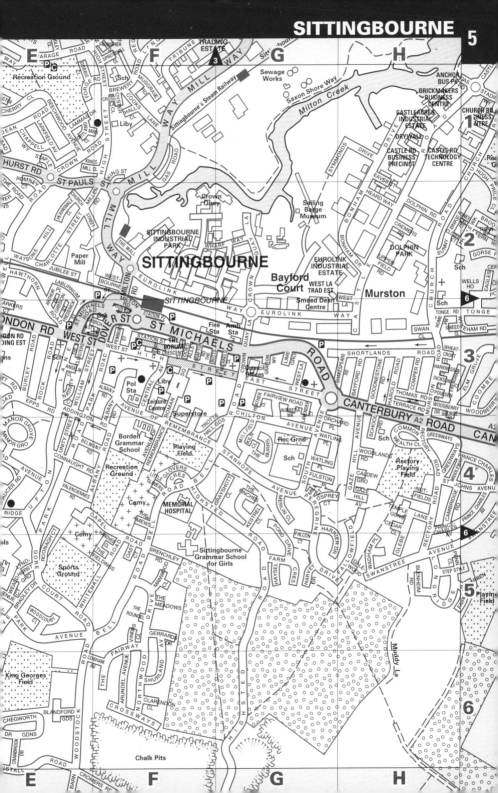

A **B** **C** **D**

Eurolink

ANCHOR
BUS-PK
ICKMAKERS
BUSINESS
CENTRE
TES

CASTLE RD
TECHNOLOGY
CENTRE

CHURCH RD
BUSINESS
CENTRE

STADIUM

Sittingbourne
Football
Club

Telegraph
Hill

BLACKETTS

1

Recreation
Ground

Mere
Court

MEERES CT

The Oast
Golf Centre

Club
House

East
Hall

West Tonge
Farm

St Giles
Houses

OAK ROAD

2

Sch

WELLS
HO

EAGLES

PORTLAND AV

CERES CT

Bunces
Farm

Sch **5**

TONGE RD

SMEED HAM RD

ALL SAINTS ROAD

TONGE   ROAD   LOMAS

ROAD

CHURCH

DRIVE

Tonge Castle
(remains of)

SCRAPS
HILL

LOWER

3

HARKNESS

DICKSONS

POULSON

WOODBERRY
DR GEORGE

ELM GROVE

COOMBE

LANSDOWN

BEACONSFIELD

SALISBURY CL
PALMERSTON
WK

GLADSTONE

LANE

ROAD

A2

WOODBERRY
AV

VINCENT

AMBLESIDE

School

ROAD

GREENWAYS

GREENWAYS

PRINCE CHARLES
AV

CANTERBURY   ROAD   FOX   HILL   THE

Snipeshill

Bapchild

STREET   LONDON   R

4

JOHNS AVENUE

CAMBRIDGE

SWANSTREE   AVENUE

PRINCE CHARLES
AV

Schs

St. Lawrence
Church

Sch

SCHOOL LA

MORRIS
COURT

ASHTEAD DR

WIHTRED

DOUBLEDAY

SCHOOL DR

HEMPSTEAD   LANE

DULLY   ROAD

Sch **5**

PRINCE
CHARLES

RECTORY   ROAD

AVENUE

STEP STILE

FARLEY

WARREN

ST.LAURENCE DR

ROAD

SCHOOL   LANE

PANTERY   LANE

Haywood

5

Playing
Field

Morris
Court

STREET

6

Little
Dully

A **B** Rodmersham **C** **D**

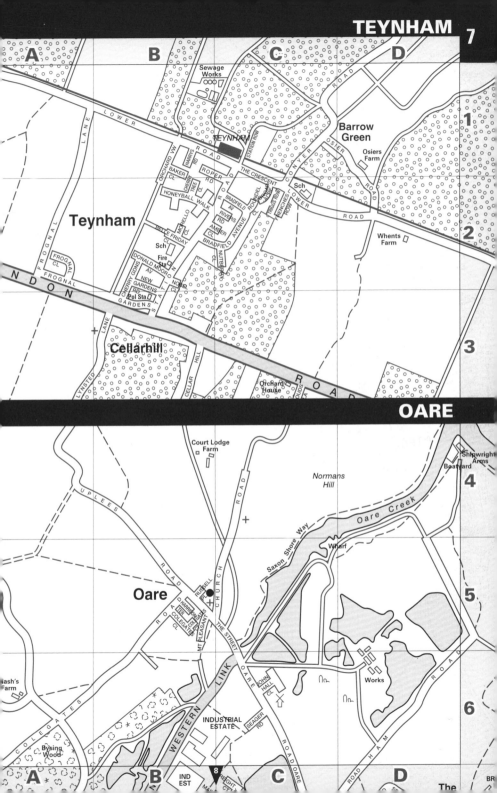

A   B   C   D

1

Sewage Works

Barrow Green

Osiers Farm

TEYNHAM

LOWER ROAD

STATION ROW

THE CRESCENT

OSIER ROAD

LOWER ROAD

Sch

ORCHARD VW

HARRIS

BAKER CL

CHERRY TREE

ROPER RD

BRADFIELD AV

ROUNDEL

THRUSTON ROW

FRENCHES ROW

Whents Farm

2

Teynham

HONEYBALL WALK

MARTELLO CL

BELLE FRIDAY CL

Sch

DONALD MOOR AV

RIVERS RD

AMBER CL

BRADFIELD

NUTBERRY

NOBEL CL

RIVERS

ROUNDEL AVENUE

FROGNAL

FROGNAL CL

FROGNAL

Fire Sta

NEW GARDENS RD

CHERRY GDNS

Pol Sta

GARDENS

L O N D O N

LYNSTED LANE

CELLAR HILL

CHURCH LANE

GOULDS RD

ROAD

3

Cellarhill

Orchard House

Court Lodge Farm

Normans Hill

Shipwright Arms

Boatyard

4

UPLEES ROAD

Oare Creek

Saxon Shore Way

Wharf

Oare

RUSSELL

HARRISON PL

COLEGATES CL

MT PLEASANT

THE STREET

CHURCH ROAD

OARE

RAM ROAD

OARE ROAD

5

Nash's Farm

JOHN HALL CL

Works

COLEGATES

WESTERN LINK

SEAGER RD

INDUSTRIAL ESTATE

FREIGHT

Bysing Wood

6

A   B   C   D

IND EST

8

The

E **F** **G** **H**

1

Faversham Creek
Saxon Shore Way
Works

2

FIELDS

Faversham

GORDON
RD CHARLES
CT
DRAYSON
CT

ABBEY
FIELDS
LUTON RD
ST
COLE RD
ABBOTS ROAD
ARDEN ROAD
CENTURY
MILLFIELD
RD
ST SAVIOURS
CT
CLUNY RD
CHENEY RD
ROAD
ABBEY
STABLE
ROAD
Swale Heritage Trail

School
Farm

3

GRAVENEY
ROAD WHITSTABLE
ROAD

LOVE LANE
Lady Dane
Farm
Cemetery

Ewell
Farm

HOMESTALL
ROAD

WINDERMERE
LES SPICKETT
CL
AMBLESIDE
ENNERDALE
BUTTERMERE
Homestall
House

4

BRAMLEY
BRAMLEY
AVENUE
NORTHDOWN RD
BLENHEIM RD
RUSSET
AV
WORCESTER
LAXTON
WY
AV

C A N T E R B U R Y
ROAD

5

MACKNADE
FARM COTTS
SELLING
Apple
Craft Centre
DESMOND CRES
Chalkpit
Hill
Brenley
Corner
LANE
ROAD
M2
JUNCTION 7

A299
A2

ROAD

6

M2
BRENLEY LANE

E **F** **G** **H**

BOUGHTON STREET

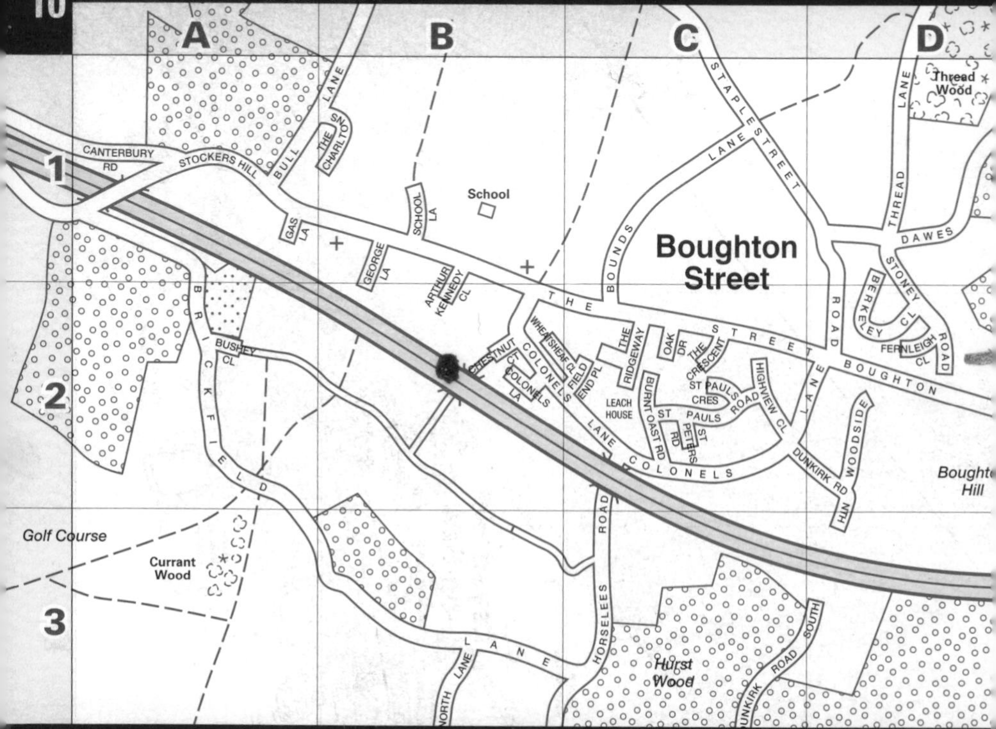
A
B
C
D
1
2
3
CANTERBURY RD
STOCKERS HILL
BULL LANE
THE CHARLTONS
GAS LA
GEORGE LA
SCHOOL LA
School
ARTHUR KENNEDY CL
BRICKFIELD
BUSHEY CL
CHESTNUT CT
COLONELS LA
WHEATSHEAF CL
FIELD END PL
THE RIDGEWAY
LEACH HOUSE
BURNT OAST RD
OAK DR
THE CRESCENT
ST PAULS CRES
ST PAULS ROAD
ST PETERS RD
HIGHVIEW CL
COLONELS LANE
THE STREET
BOUNDS LANE
STAPLE STREET
Boughton Street
ROAD
LANE
THREAD LANE
Thread Wood
DAWES
STONEY ROAD
BERKELEY CL
FERNLEIGH CL
BOUGHTON
DUNKIRK RD
WOODSIDE
NTH
Golf Course
Currant Wood
NORTH LANE
HORSELEES ROAD
Hurst Wood
DUNKIRK ROAD SOUTH

EASTCHURCH

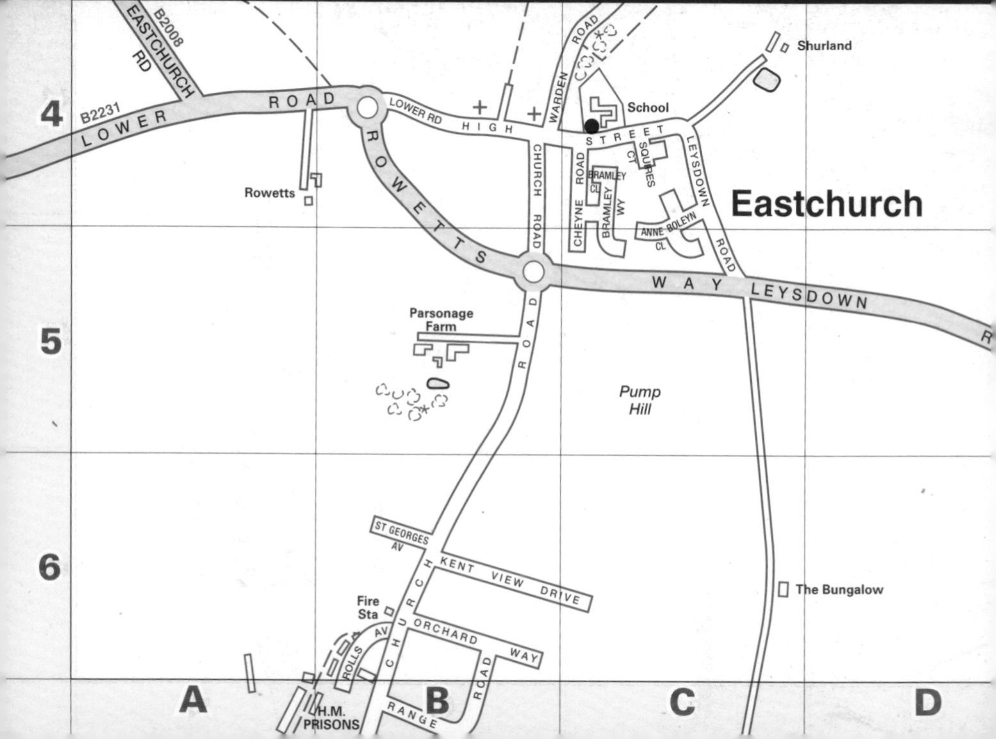
B2008 EASTCHURCH RD
B2231 LOWER ROAD
LOWER RD
HIGH STREET
WARDEN ROAD
School
Shurland
Rowetts
ROWETTS WAY
CHURCH ROAD
CHEYNE ROAD
BRAMLEY CL
BRAMLEY WY
SQUIRES CT
LEYSDOWN ROAD
ANNE BOLEYN CL
Eastchurch
LEYSDOWN RD
Parsonage Farm
Pump Hill
4
5
6
ST GEORGES AV
KENT VIEW DRIVE
The Bungalow
Fire Sta
ROLLS AV
ORCHARD WAY
CHURCH ROAD
RANGE ROAD
H.M. PRISONS
A
B
C
D

LEYSDOWN-ON-SEA

Leysdown
-on-Sea

Warden

Bay View

Thorn Hill

The Bay

Leysdown Coastal Park

Football Ground

Nutts Caravan Site

Bus Depot

Priory Hill Camp

South Bank Holiday Camp

Harts Holiday Camp

Pol Sta

Eastern Holiday Camp

Loves Holiday Camp

Sheppey Holiday Camp

Vanity Farm Holiday Camp

Happy Valley

Boating Lake

Warden Bay Hotel

Seaview Holiday Camp

Warden Bay Caravan Park

Warden Bay Holiday Camp

Coronation Chalet Camp

St Clements Church

SHURLAND AV
SEAVIEW AV
WING
SHELLNESS ROAD
PARK AV
PRIORY CL
PARK AV
MANOR WAY
NUTTS CT
PROMENADE
THE AV
EASTERN
GROVE AV
SAND CT
THAMES CT
LEYSDOWN ROAD
PARADISE GARDENS

BAY ROAD
WARDEN ROAD
JETTY
CLIFF DRIVE
ST JAMES DRIVE
SEA SALTER CL
CLIFF VW
MELODY
EMERALD
CONDOR CL
GDNS
SEA VIEW CL
CLARENCE GDNS
BEACH ROAD
LEICESTER GDNS
ST CLEMENTS GDNS
IMPERIAL CL
WINDSOR GDNS
EMPRESS GDNS
PRESTON HALL GDNS
HILL SEA
KNOLL WAY
CLIFF
APPROACH

MUSTARDS
OCEAN TER
CORONATION DR
ST CLEMENTS ROAD
BAY VIEW GARDENS
CLIFF VW GDNS
WARDEN VIEW GARDENS
DANES DRIVE
DANES DR
LEYSDOWN ROAD
B2231

Minster

East End

Minster Marshes

Scrapsgate

Merryman's Hill

Minster Park

Ripney Hill Farm

Round Hill

Royal Oak Point

Seacliff Caravan Park

Pigtail Corner

Breakneck Hill

Health Centre

Tadwell Farm

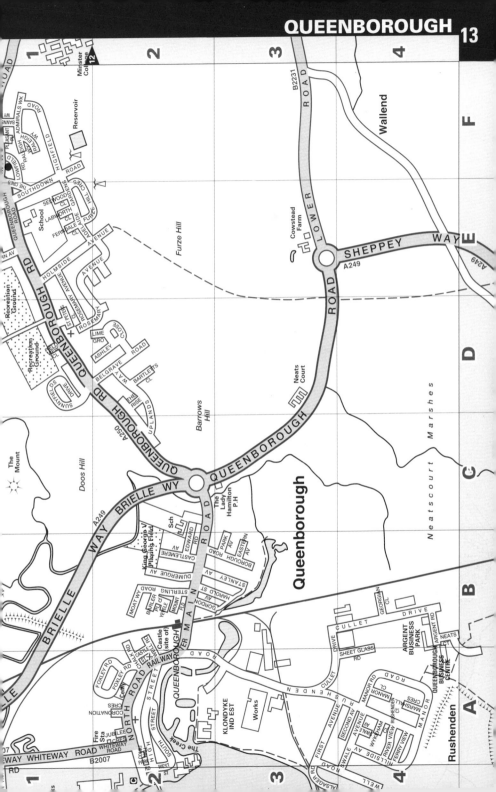

Queenborough

Rushenden

A B C D

1

Garrison Point

Garrison
Point
Fort

Lifeboat
Station

Docks

BOAT HOUSE

GARRISON

Jacobs
Bank

ESPLANADE

2

RIVER   MEDWAY

Blue
Town

ANCHOR
ROAD

PADDOCK

MAIN

GREAT BASIN RD

MORTIMER

JETTY

WEST

HIGH   STREET

UNION

CHARLES

EAST LA

BRIELLE WAY

Supersore

Amusement
Sheppey Park
College

Sports &
Leisure Centre

BEACHER

ROW

CLARENCE RD

BELLAMARK RD

HIGH ST

BROADWAY

TRINITY RD

P C

Bus
Sta

Pol
Sta

Steel Works

SHEERNESS
ON-SEA

Festival
Playing Fields

BRIDGE RD

RAILWAY

SHORT

RUSSELL

HOPE ST

ROSE RD

GRANVILLE

MILLENNIUM   WAY

Council
Offices
Lby

3

Piers

The
Lappel

Sheerness

NEW RD
INDUSTRIAL
ESTATE

GRACE RD

NEW
KENT
RD

NEW
THAMES

MEDWAY

FLEET

ESTUARY

ROAD

Sch

AVENUE

AVENUE

CECIL

SWALE

NORE CL

HOLLAND
CL

BOTANY

Mile
Town

GEORGES

VICTORIA

SECOND   AVENUE

ST AGNES

FIRST

VICTORIA

STREET

SHRUBCOTE

VINCENT

GARDENS

MAP

4

MILE TOWN
INDUSTRIAL
ESTATE

DORSET
RD

DORSET RD
INDUSTRIAL
ESTATE

NELSON
CL

The Fleet

BRIDGE WATER RD

MINERVA
CT

BRITON
CT

BRONT

SHEARWATER
CT

MONTAGUE

CARLTON
AV

WHEATSHEAF
GDNS

Sports
Ground

SOUTHVIEW

GARD

SHEPPEY CO
MARSHES

5

West Minster

BRIELLE WAY

NEW

WAY

QUEENS

DRIVE

COATS AV

LINDEN
RD

NEWLAND
RD

QUEENS
WAY

CHERRY
TREE CT

ALMOND
TREE CL

HAWTHORN   AVENUE

LARCH
CL

ALDER
CT

ST GEORGES

DAVIE CL

MILE CT

Sch

Sch

EDENBRIDGE

MILSTED
CL

CHILHAM

APPLEDORE

EDENBRIDGE
DR

BOXLEY DR

HARTLIP
CL

BREDHURST

DETLING
CL

Diggs   Marshes

6

BRIELLE
WAY

A249

B2007

PIER ROAD

WHITEWAY   WHIT

The
Mount

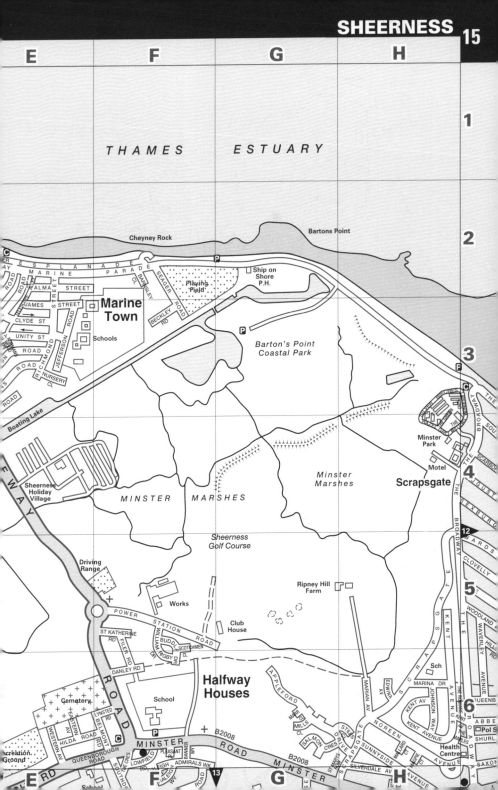

E   **F**   **G**   **H**

1

THAMES   ESTUARY

2

Cheyney Rock   Bartons Point

ESPLANADE
MARINE   PARADE
ALMA STREET
JAMES   STREET
BARSLEY
SEAGER ROAD
BECKLEY RD
Playing Field
Ship on Shore P.H.

Marine Town

CLYDE ST
UNITY ST
Schools
JEFFERSON ROAD
RICHMOND
NURSERY CL

Barton's Point Coastal Park

Boating Lake

3

Minster Park

THE BROADWAY
THE SCARBOR
C

Minster Marshes

Scrapsgate

Motel

4

THE AUGUST

THE SEXBURG

MINSTER   MARSHES

Sheerness Holiday Village

12

BROADWAY

Sheerness Golf Course

CLOVELLY

Driving Range

WOODLAND

WAVERLEY

Ripney Hill Farm

5

THE

KENT

AVENUE

HILLS

Works

Club House

Sch

KENT AV

6

St Katherine RD
POWER STATION ROAD
FILER RD
WILLIAM RIGBY DRI
BUDD
SCOTCHMEN CL

MARIAN AV

EDWINA

MARINA DR

KENT AV

JOHNSON WAY

KENT AVENUE

QUEENB

DANLEY RD

Halfway Houses

School

APPLEFORD

NOREEN

AVENUE

ABBE

SHURL

ROAD

Cemetery

LYNSTED
BELMONT
EASTERN AV
WESTERN AV
HILDA ROAD

MARR MILLS
SALMON CRES

STEEL DRIVE
SCRAPSGATE

SUNNYSIDE

Pol S

Health Centre

SAXON

B2008

MINSTER   ROAD

Lowfield
PLEASANT
BANNER
ROTHLEIGH
ADMIRALS WK

QUEENBOROUGH ROAD

13

SILVERDALE AV

ecreation Ground

School

F   **G**   **H**

B2008

The Index includes some names for which there is insufficient space on the maps. These names are indicated by an * and are followed by the nearest adjoining thoroughfare.

Preston St ME13 — 8 D3
Primrose La ME9 — 17 E6
Prince Charles Av, Sheerness ME12 — 12 D4
Prince Charles Av, Sittingbourne ME10 — 6 A4
Princes Av ME12 — 12 D3
Priory Ct ME12 — 11 E4
Priory Pl ME13 — 8 C1
Priory Rd ME13 — 8 C2
Priory Row ME13 — 8 C1
Puttney Dr ME10 — 3 E3

Quay La ME13 — 8 D2
Queenborough Dr ME12 — 12 B3
Queenborough Rd ME12 — 13 C2
Queens Rd, Faversham ME13 — 8 B3
Queens Rd, Sheerness ME12 — 12 D3
Queens Way ME12 — 14 B5
Quickstep Cl ME10 — 3 D3
Quinton Rd ME10 — 3 A3

Railway Rd ME12 — 14 C3
Railway Ter ME11 — 13 A2
Raleigh Way ME12 — 13 F1
Ranelagh Rd ME12 — 14 D2
Recreation Way ME10 — 3 E2
Rectory Rd ME10 — 5 H5
Red Robin Cotts ME9 — 17 E7
Reedland Cres ME13 — 8 C1
Regency Ct ME10 — 5 E2
Regis Cres ME10 — 3 D4
Rettendon Dr ME10 — 3 D3
Rhode Ct ME10 — 4 D2
Richmond Dr ME10 — 3 D4
Richmond St ME12 — 15 E3
Riddles Rd ME10 — 4 C4
Ridham Av ME10 — 3 E2
River Vw ME11 — 13 A4
Riverhead Cl ME10 — 4 D4
Rivers Rd ME9 — 7 C2
Roberts Cl ME10 — 3 C4
Rock Rd ME10 — 5 E3
Rodmer Cl ME12 — 12 C2
Roebuck Rd ME13 — 8 A3
Rolls Av ME12 — 10 B6
Rolvenden Dr ME10 — 4 C2
Roman Rd ME13 — 8 C3
Roman Sq ME10 — 5 F3
Romney Ct ME10 — 5 E1
Rook La ME9 — 4 A1
Roonagh Ct ME10 — 5 E5
Roper Rd ME9 — 7 B1
Rose Ct ME9 — 17 D6
Rose St ME12 — 14 C3
Rosebery Cl ME10 — 6 B3
Roseleigh Rd ME10 — 4 D6
Rosemary Av ME12 — 13 D1
Roundel Cl ME9 — 7 C2
Rowetts Way ME12 — 10 B4
Royal Rd ME12 — 14 D2
Ruby Cl ME10 — 3 B4
Rule Ct ME12 — 14 C4
Runnymede Mews ME13 — 13 A4
Rushenden Cl ME11 — 13 A4
Rushenden Rd ME11 — 13 A4
Russell Cl ME10 — 4 C4
Russell Pl ME13 — 7 B5
Russell St ME12 — 14 C3
Russet Av ME13 — 9 E4

Saffron Way ME10 — 3 E4
St Agnes Gdns ME12 — 14 D4
St Anns Rd ME13 — 8 B3
St Catherines Dr ME13 — 8 D4
St Clements Cl ME12 — 11 B3
St Clements Rd ME12 — 11 B2
St Georges Av, Eastchurch ME12 — 10 B6
St Georges Av, Sheerness ME12 — 14 C5
St Georges Ct ME12 — 14 C4
St Helens Rd ME12 — 15 E3
St James Cl ME12 — 11 B1
St Johns Av ME10 — 5 H4
St Johns Rd ME13 — 8 D3
St Katherine Rd ME12 — 15 F5
St Laurence Cl ME9 — 6 B5
St Marks Cl ME9 — 17 E6
St Martins Cl ME9 — 17 E6
St Marys Pl ME9 — 17 E6
St Marys Rd ME12 — 8 B3
St Marys Row ME12 — 12 A3
St Marys Vw ME9 — 17 E6
St Matthews Cl ME9 — 17 E6
St Michaels Cl ME9 — 5 G3
St Michaels Rd ME10 — 5 F3

St Nicholas Rd ME13 — 8 A3
St Pauls Av ME13 — 8 A3
St Pauls Cres ME13 — 10 C2
St Pauls Rd ME13 — 10 C2
St Pauls St ME10 — 5 E2
St Peters Cl ME13 — 13 D1
St Peters Ct ME13 — 8 C3
St Peters Rd ME13 — 10 C2
St Saviours Cl ME13 — 9 E3
St Stephens Cl ME9 — 17 E6
Salisbury Cl ME10 — 6 A3
Salmon Cres ME12 — 12 A3
Salters La ME13 — 8 D6
Sand Ct ME12 — 11 D3
Sanders Ct ME12 — 12 A4
Sandford Rd ME10 — 4 B2
Sandstone Dr ME10 — 3 D2
Sanspareil Av ME12 — 12 A4
Satis Av ME10 — 3 D4
Saxon Av ME12 — 12 B3
Saxon Rd ME13 — 8 C3
Scarborough Dr ME12 — 12 B1
School La, Bapchild ME9 — 6 B4
School La, Borden ME9 — 4 A3
School La, Faversham ME13 — 10 B1
School La, Lower Halstow ME9 — 16 E3
School La, Newington ME9 — 17 D5
School Rd, Faversham ME13 — 8 B3
School Rd, Sittingbourne ME10 — 5 H4
Scotles Rd ME12 — 12 C4
Scotchmen Cl ME12 — 15 F5
Scraps Hill ME9 — 6 C3
Scrapsgate ME12 — 12 A3
Sea App ME12 — 11 B1
Sea View Gdns ME12 — 11 B2
Seager Rd, Faversham ME13 — 7 C6
Seager Rd, Sheerness ME12 — 15 F2
Seasalter Cl ME12 — 11 C1
Seaside Av ME12 — 12 C2
Seathorpe Av ME12 — 12 D2
Seaview Av ME12 — 11 F4
Second Av, Queenborough ME11 — 13 A4
Second Av, Sheerness ME12 — 14 C4
Selling Rd ME13 — 9 E5
Selwood Cl ME12 — 13 E1
Sevenacre Rd ME13 — 8 C1
Sexburga Dr ME12 — 12 B1
Shakespeare Rd ME10 — 5 H3
Shearwater Ct ME12 — 14 C4
Sheerness Rd ME9 — 16 E2
Sheerways ME13 — 8 A3
Sheet Glass Rd ME13 — 13 A4
Shellness Rd ME12 — 11 E4
Sheppey St ME12 — 14 B2
Sheppey Way, Sheerness ME12 — 13 E4
Sheppey Way, Sittingbourne ME9 — 4 A2
Sherwood Cl ME13 — 8 B1
Short St ME12 — 14 C2
Shortlands Rd ME10 — 5 H3
Shrubsole Av ME12 — 14 D3
Shurland Av, Leysdown-on-Sea ME12 — 11 E4
Shurland Av, Minster ME12 — 12 B3
Shurland Av, Sittingbourne ME10 — 5 F6
Silver Birches ME12 — 15 H4
Silverdale Av ME12 — 12 A3
Silverdale Gro ME10 — 4 D3
Simpson Rd ME10 — 4 C2
Slipway Rd ME12 — 14 B1
Smack Alley ME13 — 8 D2
Smeed Cl ME10 — 5 H3
Solomans La ME13 — 8 D3
Somerset Cl ME10 — 4 C3
Sonora Way ME10 — 4 C1
South Av ME10 — 5 G4
South Rd ME13 — 8 C3
South St ME11 — 13 A2
Southdown Rd ME12 — 13 E1
Southsea Av ME12 — 12 B1
Southview Gdns ME12 — 14 D4
Spillett Cl ME13 — 8 C3
Springfield Rd ME10 — 4 D2
Springhead Rd ME13 — 8 C1
Sprotshill Cl ME12 — 3 D4
Squires Ct ME12 — 10 C4
Stable Ct ME13 — 8 D3

Stadium Way ME10 — 6 A1
Stanhope Av ME10 — 5 G4
Stanley Av, Queenborough ME11 — 13 B3
Stanley Av, Sheerness ME12 — 12 E3
Staple Cl ME10 — 5 E1
Staplehurst Rd ME10 — 4 C1
Staplestreet Rd ME13 — 10 C1
Station Pl ME10 — 5 F3
Station Rd, Faversham ME13 — 8 D3
Station Rd, Newington ME9 — 17 E7
Station Rd, Teynham ME9 — 7 B3
Station Row ME9 — 7 C1
Station St ME10 — 5 F3
Step Style ME13 — 5 H5
Stephens Cl ME13 — 8 B2
Sterling Rd, Queenborough ME11 — 13 B2
Sterling Rd, Sittingbourne ME10 — 4 D6
Stickfast La ME10 — 3 A2
Stiles Cl ME12 — 12 A3
Stockers Hill ME13 — 10 A1
Stone St ME13 — 8 C3
Stonebridge Way ME13 — 8 B3
Stonedane Ct ME13 — 8 C1
Stoney Rd ME13 — 10 D1
Strode Cres ME12 — 14 D2
Summerville Av ME12 — 12 A4
Summerville Cl*, Gordon Sq ME13 — 9 E2
Sumpter Way ME13 — 8 A2
Sunny Bank ME12 — 5 H2
Sunnyfields Dr ME12 — 13 D1
Sunnyside Ct ME12 — 12 A3
Susans La ME9 — 16 C2
Swale Av, Queenborough ME11 — 13 A4
Swale Av, Sheerness ME12 — 14 C3
Swan Cl ME10 — 5 H3
Swanstree Av ME10 — 5 H5
Sydney Av ME10 — 4 D3
Symmonds Dr ME10 — 5 G1

Taillour Cl ME10 — 3 E3
Tams Gdns ME12 — 12 E3
Tanners St ME13 — 8 C3
Tavistock Cl ME10 — 4 D3
Telescope Alley ME12 — 15 E3
Temple Gdns ME12 — 5 H4
Tenby Ct ME13 — 8 C3
Terrace Rd ME10 — 5 H3
Thames Av ME12 — 14 C3
Thames Ct ME12 — 11 D3
The Broadway ME12 — 12 B1
The Burrs ME10 — 5 G4
The Butts ME10 — 5 F3
The Charltons ME13 — 10 B1
The Cloisters ME13 — 5 E3
The Close ME13 — 8 C4
The Crescent, Faversham ME13 — 10 C2
The Crescent, Kemsley ME10 — 3 E2
The Crescent, Sheerness ME12 — 13 E1
The Crescent, Teynham ME9 — 7 C1
The Fairway ME10 — 5 F6
The Fieldings ME10 — 5 F5
The Finches ME10 — 5 G4
The Forum ME10 — 5 F3
The Glen ME12 — 12 B,C2
The Green, Sheerness ME12 — 15 H4
The Green, Sittingbourne ME9 — 16 D2
The Knole ME13 — 8 B2
The Larches ME13 — 8 A2
The Leas ME13 — 8 B2
The Mall ME13 — 8 C4
The Maltings ME13 — 8 D1
The Maples ME12 — 12 B3
The Meadows ME10 — 4 D5
The Meads Av ME10 — 3 B4
The Mews ME10 — 5 F4
The Poles ME9 — 16 B1
The Promenade ME13 — 11 E3
The Ridgeway ME13 — 10 C2
The Rise, Sheerness ME12 — 13 D2
The Rise, Sittingbourne ME9 — 4 C5
The Roundel ME10 — 5 F5
The Rowans ME12 — 12 B3

The Square ME10 — 3 E2
The Street, Bapchild ME9 — 6 B4
The Street, Borden ME9 — 4 B4
The Street, Boughton Street ME13 — 10 B2
The Street, Hartlip ME9 — 17 A8
The Street, Lower Halstow ME9 — 16 D2
The Street, Oare ME13 — 7 C5
The Street, Upchurch ME9 — 16 B2
The Tracies ME10 — 17 E7
The Wall ME10 — 5 F2
The Willows, Kemsley ME10 — 3 E2
The Willows, Newington ME9 — 17 D7
The Willows, Sheerness ME12 — 15 H4
Thistle Hill Way ME12 — 12 C4
Thistle Walk ME10 — 6 A2
Thomas Rd, Faversham ME13 — 8 C2
Thomas Rd, Sittingbourne ME10 — 5 H3
Thorn Hill Rd ME12 — 11 B1
Thorn Walk ME10 — 6 A2
Thread La ME13 — 10 D1
Todd Cres ME10 — 3 F3
Tonge Rd ME10 — 5 H3
Tourmaline Dr ME10 — 3 B4
Tribune Ct ME10 — 14 C4
Tribune Dr ME10 — 3 D4
Triggs Row ME9 — 7 C2
Trinity Pl ME12 — 14 D2
Trinity Rd, Sheerness ME12 — 14 D2
Trinity Rd, Sittingbourne ME10 — 3 E4
Trotts Hall Gdns ME10 — 5 F4
Tunstall Rd ME10 — 5 E6
Turmine Ct ME12 — 12 A4
Turner Cl ME10 — 3 E3
Turners Cl ME12 — 14 D3
Tysoe Ct ME12 — 12 A4

Ufton La ME10 — 5 H5
Union Rd ME12 — 12 D3
Union Rd, Faversham ME13 — 8 D3
Union St, Sheerness ME12 — 14 B2
Unity St, Sheerness ME12 — 15 E3
Unity St, Sittingbourne ME10 — 5 E4
Uplands Way ME12 — 13 C2
Uplees Rd ME13 — 7 A4
Upper Brents ME13 — 8 D2
Upper Field Rd ME10 — 5 H2
Upper St Anns Rd ME13 — 8 B4

Valenciennes Rd ME10 — 5 H5
Van Rd ME10 — 5 F3
Vaughan Dr ME10 — 3 E3
Vectis Dr ME10 — 3 D3
Vicarage Cl ME10 — 17 E6
Vicarage La, Faversham ME13 — 8 A4
Vicarage La, Sittingbourne ME9 — 16 E2
Vicarage Rd, Sheerness ME12 — 12 D3
Vicarage Rd, Sittingbourne ME10 — 3 C4
Vicarage St ME10 — 3 D2
Victoria Pl ME13 — 8 C3
Victoria Rd ME10 — 4 D2
Victoria St ME12 — 14 D4
Victory St ME12 — 14 C2
Vincent Ct ME12 — 14 D4
Vincent Gdns ME12 — 14 D4
Vincent Rd ME10 — 6 A3
Viners Cl ME10 — 5 F5
Volante Dr ME10 — 3 C4

Wadham Pl ME10 — 5 H5
Wallbridge La ME9 — 16 A3
Wallers Rd ME13 — 8 A3
Walmer Gdns ME10 — 5 E2
Walnut Tree Dr ME10 — 4 D3
Walsby Dr ME10 — 3 F3
Warden Bay Rd ME12 — 11 C2
Warden Rd ME12 — 10 B4
Warden View Gdns ME12 — 11 A4
Wards Hill Rd ME12 — 12 B1
Wardwell La ME9 — 17 E6
Warren Cl ME10 — 6 A5
Warwick Cres ME10 — 4 C2

Water La, Faversham ME13
Water La, Ospringe ME13
Waterloo Hill ME12
Waterloo Rd ME10
Waterside ME13
Waterside Vw ME12
Watling Pl ME10
Watsons Hill ME10
Waverley Av ME12
Weald Ct ME10
Well Rd ME11
Wellesley Rd ME12
Wellington Rd ME10
Wells Ho ME10
Wells Way ME13
Wellwinch Rd ME12
Wentworth Dr ME10
West Grn ME10
West La, Sheerness ME12
West La, West La Trading E[state], Sittingbourne ME10
West La, East St, Sittingbourne ME10
West Ridge ME10
West St, Faversham ME13
West St, Sheerness ME12
West St, Westbourne St ME10
Westcliff Dr ME12
Westerham Rd ME10
Western Av ME12
Western Link ME13
Westgate Rd ME13
Westlands Av ME10
Westmoreland Dr ME9
Westwood Pl ME13
Westwood Walk ME9
Wharf Way ME10
Wheatcroft Cl ME10
Wheatsheaf Cl ME13
Wheatsheaf Gdns ME12
Whimbrel Cl ME10
Whitehall Rd ME10
Whiteway Rd ME11
Whiting Cres ME13
Whitstable Rd, Faversham ME13
Whitstable Rd, Faversham ME13
Whybornes Chase ME12
Wickham Cl ME10
Wihtred Rd ME9
Wildish Rd ME13
Willement Rd ME13
William Rigby Dr ME12
William St, Faversham ME13
William St, Sittingbourne ME10
Willis Ct ME12
Willow Av ME13
Wilton Ter ME10
Windermere ME13
Windermere Gro ME10
Windmill Rd ME10
Windmill Rise ME12
Windsor Dr ME10
Windsor Gdns ME12
Wing Rd ME12
Winstanley Rd ME12
Wises La ME10
Wood St ME12
Woodberry Dr ME10
Woodcourt ME10
Woodgate Cl ME13
Woodland Dr ME12
Woodlands Rd ME10
Woodside ME13
Woodside Gdns ME10
Woodstock Rd ME10
Woollett Rd ME10
Worcester Cl, Faversham ME13
Worcester Cl, Sheerness ME12
Worcester Dr ME10
Wreight Ct ME13
Wykeham Cl ME11
Wykeham Rd ME10
Wyllie Ct ME12
Wyvern Cl ME10

Yeates Dr ME10
Yevele Cl ME11
Ypres Dr ME10